Published by
Lion Hudson Limited
Wilkinson House, Jordan Hill Business Park
Banbury Road, Oxford OX2 8DR, England
www.lionhudson.com

ISBN 978 0 7459 7797 3

First edition 2021

A catalogue record for this book is available from the British Library

Printed and bound in China, February 2021, LH54

Albert and the Journey Home

A Parable of Jesus

Written by Richard Littledale
Illustrated by Heather Heyworth

LION CHILDREN'S

"I'm leaving," squeaked Simon mouse at the top of his very small voice. "It's no fun here!" His fury made his whiskers twitch, and his tail had tied itself into a teeny-tiny knot.

Just then, Albert put out a paw to stop him. “Not so fast, young mouselet,” he said. “Let me tell you a story passed down to me by a very wise old mouse. If you still want to go after that, then so be it.

"Long ago, two boys lived on a farm with their dad, their cows and sheep – and a family of mice as well. On some days the boys helped with the ploughing.

On some days they helped with herding the sheep, and on some days they helped with the stinky, smelly job of cleaning out the barn.

"For the mice, the best job was when the boys brought the corn into the barn. They would drop lots of pieces behind them and the mice would have a feast.

"One day, the youngest son had had enough. First he got bored,

then he got *really* bored,

then he sulked,

then he puffed . . .

"… and at last he decided to tell his dad all about it.

"'Dad,' he said, 'I've had enough. I can't stand it any more. One day, when you are gone, I'll get some of your golden coins. So can't I just have them now and leave?'"

Simon nodded eagerly at the thought of that.

"His dad looked sad and his brother looked shocked. But the father handed over the jangling coins in a little cloth bag.

"With that, the younger brother took off like a rocket. He couldn't wait to leave the cows and sheep, the plough, the farm, and his brother all behind.

“As fast as his legs would carry him, he headed for the city and began to spend all the gold coins in his bag. He bought everything he wanted and he made new friends. But his new friends only wanted his money, and so he bought things they wanted too.”

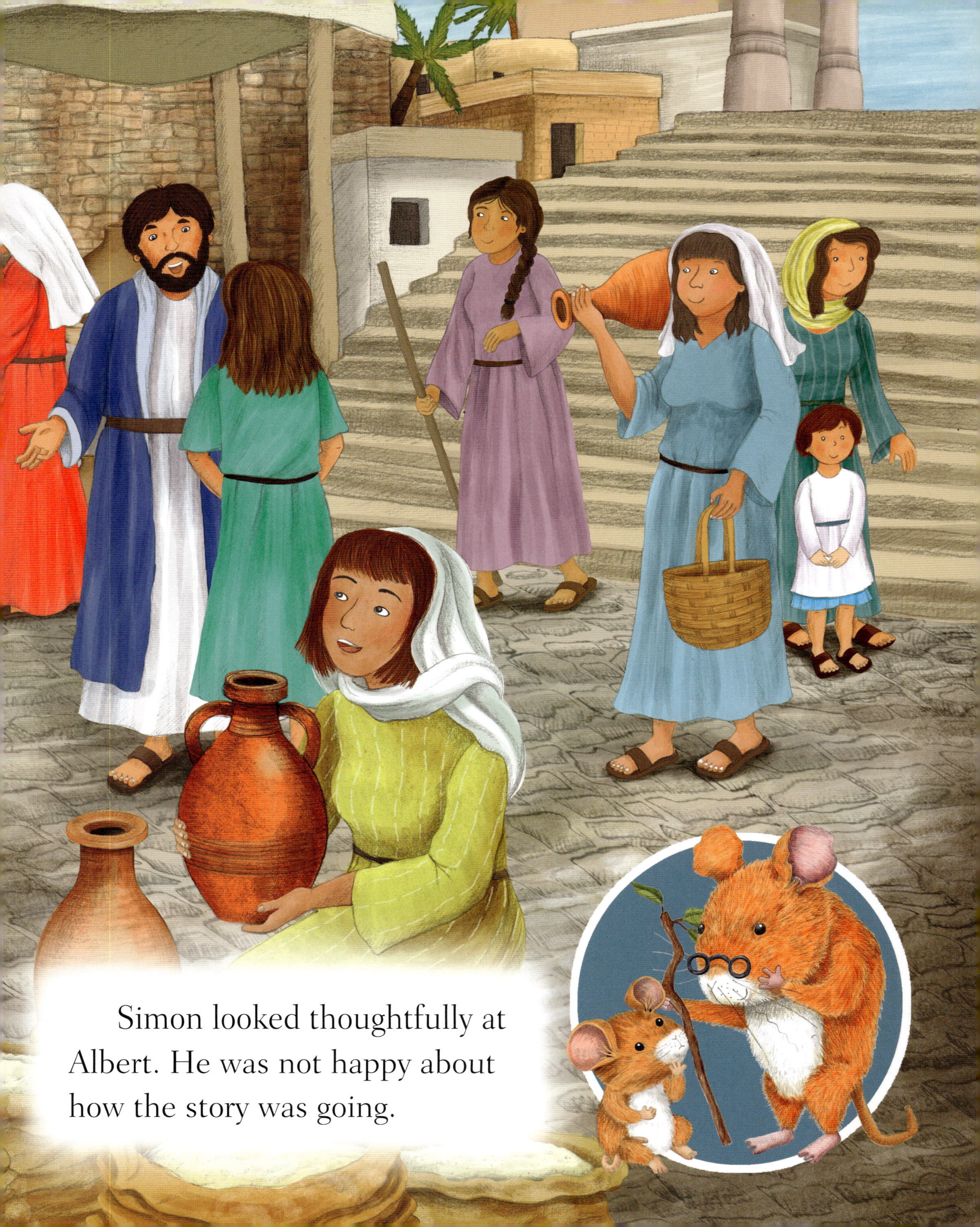

Simon looked thoughtfully at Albert. He was not happy about how the story was going.

"Before long," Albert continued, "the boy reached into his bag to pay for the next thing, and there was nothing left. Not a single coin!

He opened it up, peeked inside, turned it upside down and shook it, but the coins were all gone. Whatever was he to do?

“To keep himself from starving,
he got a job on another farm,
looking after the pigs.

“There were four of them, and he named them Noff, Oink, Snuffle, and Grunt. Each day he would care for them, and some days he thought they looked better cared for than he did.

"'Oh piggies,' the boy said to them one day, 'whatever shall I do?'

"They turned to him with their muddy pink noses.

"'Noff!' said Noff.

"'Oink!' said Oink.

"'Grunt!' said Grunt.

"And Snuffle just turned away and snuffled."

"Turn away and go home," said Simon, so caught up in the story that he didn't realise he had said it out loud.

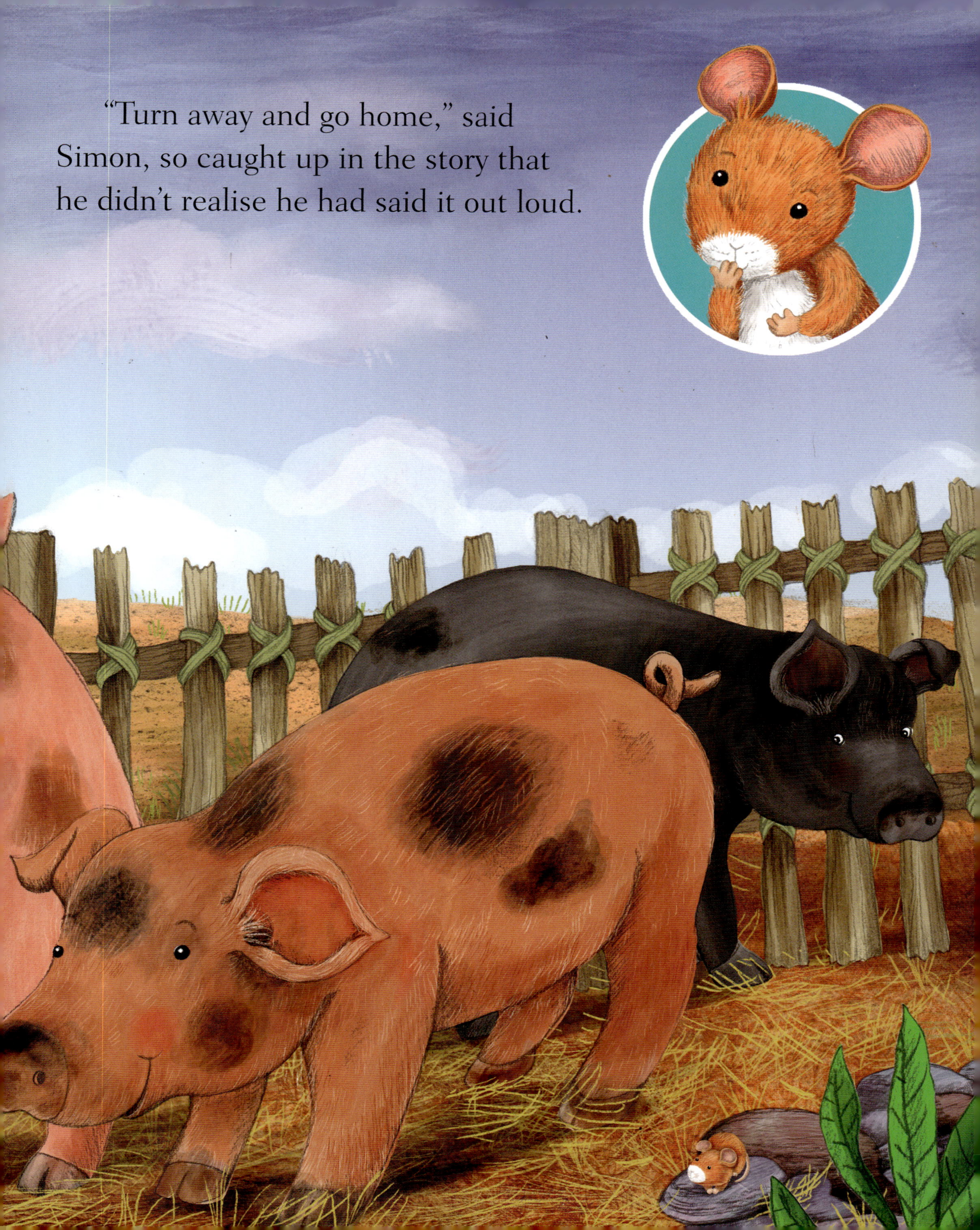

Albert nodded. "'Turn away,' thought the boy. 'That's what I shall do. I'll turn away from all the silly mistakes I've made and I'll go back home to Dad.'

"Waving goodbye to the pigs,
he set off back down the road.

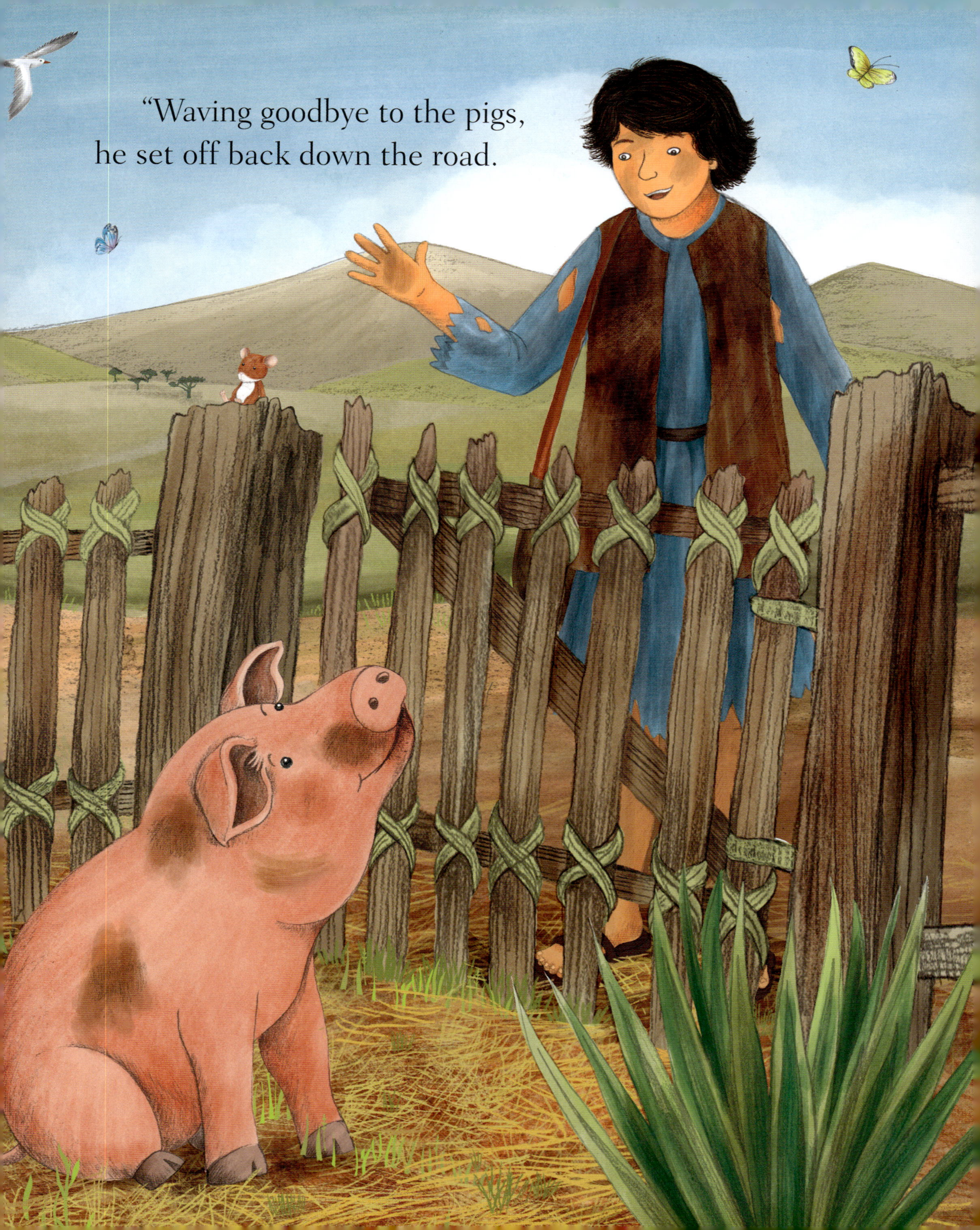

“As he got closer to home, his heart started to beat a little faster. ‘Whatever will Dad say,’ he wondered. ‘Will he be really, really cross?’

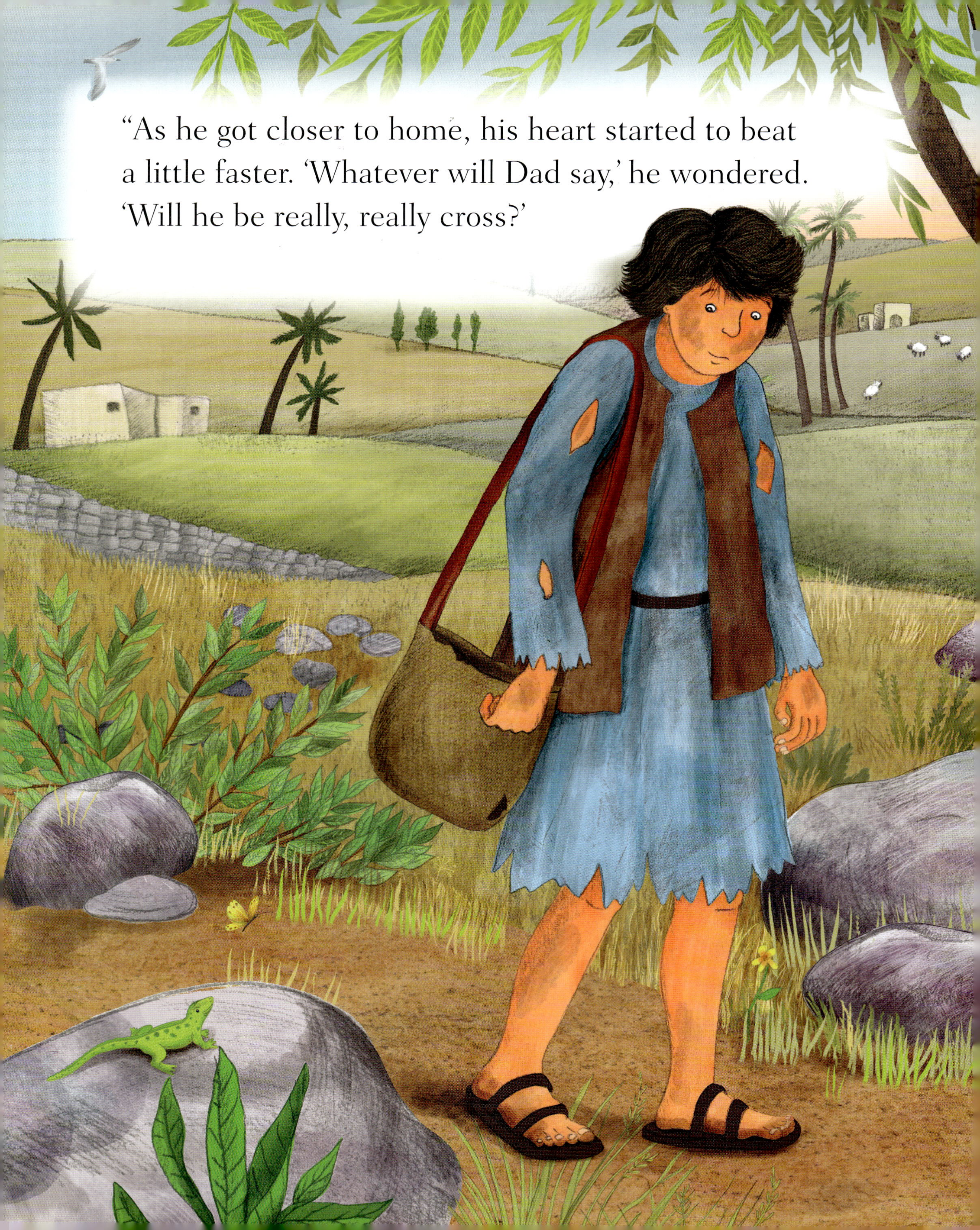

“The boy needn’t have worried. Just as he rounded the last bend in the road, he could see a figure waiting outside the farm.

It was his dad, looking out down the road, with his hand across his eyes to see if maybe today would be the day when his lovely boy came home.

"When the two of them spotted each other, they both ran as fast as they could. The boy ran quickly on his young legs, and the dad a bit slower on his old ones. When they met up, they had the biggest hug you can ever imagine."

Albert stopped his tale, and looked down at Simon. Simon was not so cross anymore.

"I think I'll just go home," he said.

Albert smiled as the knot in Simon's tail came undone.

Jesus told that story about his dad, and you can find it in the Bible in the Gospel of Luke.